LEAVE NO WAY OUT!

A GUIDE TO GETTING AND STAYING MARRIED

TIFFANY MARSH

WESTBOW
PRESS®
A DIVISION OF THOMAS NELSON
& ZONDERVAN

WestBow Press books may be ordered through booksellers or by contacting:

WestBow Press
A Division of Thomas Nelson & Zondervan
1663 Liberty Drive
Bloomington, IN 47403
www.westbowpress.com
1 (866) 928-1240

ISBN: 978-1-9736-2818-7 (sc)
ISBN: 978-1-9736-2817-0 (hc)
ISBN: 978-1-9736-2819-4 (e)

Library of Congress Control Number: 2018905532

Print information available on the last page.

WestBow Press rev. date: 05/22/2018

In loving memory of my son Tomas; I miss you.

This book is dedicated to my children Cheyenna, Ka'Teanna and Elijah when they consider marriage to people of God.

May all of you read this book and consider these questions and statements with your whole heart before you take your vows before the Lord.

To My husband Michael Marsh, I love you and may God continue blessing our marriage for many more years.

CONTENTS

PROLOGUE

A familiar quote says, "The difficult we do immediately; the impossible takes a little longer." Marriage is the sanctity of two people who love each other. It is an eternal commitment among you, your spouse, and God. Getting married is a very serious decision; sadly, it is not always taken as such in America. Getting married is easy; staying married is where faith comes in.

According to the Bible, marriage is the closest example of the relationship between God and his believers, the church. With Christ as the groom and we believers as his bride, we can never fail. However, when we attempt to do marriage without God, it will most likely be the most unpleasant, trying adventure in your life, one that will likely fail.

Christians get married (and divorced) for the same reasons as nonbelievers. Marriage is under attack. This statement is not unheard of throughout the world; however, the idea that Christians are divorcing at the same rate as nonbelievers is inexcusable. When Christians appear to be getting divorced like those who are in the world, is a sign that our faith walk is wayward and self-seeking. Our approach to marriage is the same. We look at ourselves and our own reasoning to both rectify and heal the troubles that plague marriage.

Think: just as no fingerprints are the same, neither is any marriage.

- ☐ All marriages are unique and should be.
- ☐ Make your marriage your own.
- ☐ You must be proud of the uniqueness of your marriage.

When husbands and wives attempt to mirror their marriage after an idea of what others believe marriage should be, their marriage has already begun to fail. The purpose of this book is to help married or engaged couples understand reasons to get and stay married. There are many reasons to get married, but only one reason the Bible allows for a divorce. When considering marriage, you must leave no way out.

A Prayer

Heavenly Father, let your written word be incased in these words. Father, before readers open this book, please open their hearts to its truth and allow them to receive its true meaning. I ask you humbly to let these words edify the ears and eyes of the reader. Speak loud and clear to help get through to readers as they make life-changing decisions. I ask all this in the name of Jesus, Amen.

An Overview

Leave No Way Out is written as a guide to help couples through the decision to get married and stay together. The book is meant to aid people who are wrestling through the dark days that sometimes occur in a relationship. When you are dealing with your spouse's issues and the different ordeals that may arise during your marriage, you may find yourself wanting out.

In a word, marriage is work; alongside of raising children, it is the most rewarding yet hardest thing a person can do in a lifetime. When thinking about getting married (or staying in your marriage), you must consider many factors; if you are considering marriage, you must first ask yourself if the two of you make sense together. Are you headed in the same direction? Are you equally yoked? Marriage is to be regarded as a lifetime decision; it is not a fad or something to do. Marriage is a vow made to God and your partner.

When most people consider marriage, they only think about their feelings of love. They often believe that they will feel this way forever. Sadly, most who consider marriage fail to realize that this is about spending a lifetime together with another person, forever, for better or for worse, in sickness and in health, for richer or poorer, till death.

If you are already married or are rethinking your marriage, reading this book may help you remain married. There are many reasons to get married, but only one reason for divorce. Therefore, you must close all the exit doors and leave no way out.

Chapter 1

When I Say, "I Do," Do I Really?

When you are deciding to get (or to remain) married, there are a lot of things to consider. For better or for worse seems to be considered last, when it should most definitely be carefully measured first. A lot of the time, my husband and I cackle and fight like two roosters in a cage. This does not happen because we do not love each other; it happens because we are different people who came from different households and have different backgrounds. I was raised by a single mother. Michael was raised in a nuclear, military family. His parents were together for forty-four years. All his siblings are married, and they've been together for over twenty-five years each. My siblings are single, and my brother and I both have been divorced. My mother was married three times. My husband is fourteen years older than I am; he is also divorced and has three grown children. I raised my four children as a single mother.

These factors already have left room for many disagreements in our marriage. Our different histories are the cause of most of the cackling. This is caused by our dissimilarities due to our upbringings. When you were asked, "Do you take this person to be your lawfully wedded spouse," you said, "Yes," or "I do." You then made a vow before God and witnesses to love and honor your spouse, in sickness and in health, for richer or poorer, till death do you part.

Do these words sound familiar?

These are the words we often think of when we think of getting married. This is an example of the vows you will make (or have made) to God, family, and friends. You stood there and examined your beloved's eyes and said, "You are it for me, the one I want, the one I accept, the one I will grow old and spend my life with." After the rings were placed on the fingers and the dancing was over, real life began.

Answer these questions:

- ☐ Is the person you vowed to love the person you want to wake up to every morning for the rest of your life?
- ☐ Is this person the one you cannot be without?
- ☐ Did you really mean "till death"?

These questioned should be asked and answered before you consider getting married.

What if you are already married? What now? The answer is to leave no way out.

In 1 Corinthians 7:15 (NLT), it says, "But if the husband or wife who isn't a believer insist on leaving, let them go. In such cases the Christian husband or wife is no-longer bound to the other, for God has called you to live in peace." If a person wants out of the marriage and they are not a believer, then there is nothing you can do to stop them from leaving. However, to you the believer, everything in your world is to be taken to God in prayer before any decision is made. (Read Philippians 4:6. NIV)

We believers are different: we think differently, we understand differently, and we love differently. Our approach to unhappiness is not like that of the nonbeliever. We are to pray without ceasing (1 Thessalonians 5:17, KJV); this means that we need to be in constant prayer over everything, always. If you don't know what to do in a situation, then you should do nothing, let go, and let God do the work. Men and women of God need to go to the word for every decision we make. If you do not know what the Bible has to say about a subject, then learn about it. 2 Timothy 2:15 (ASV) says, "Study to show thy self-approved" … What I am saying is, don't decide for yourself; get a Bible Concordance, or research it.

Whatever decision you make, make sure that it lines up with the word of God. Marriage is sacred, and if you've chosen to take this step, then you should close all the doors behind you. You've said goodbye to other personal relationships that are not going to be a blessing in your marriage. You also must learn to reprioritize your relationships with other relatives: parents, siblings, and, yes, your children. Genesis 2:24 says, that we are to leave and cleave. You must reassess those who were a priority in your former life. Your focus has now become your spouse. Meeting his or her needs and feelings is what's now important.

Note: You are not responsible for the happiness of

your mate. You are only responsible for your happiness. You are also responsible for your words and your actions.

No one person can make another person happy. Happiness comes from within, and it revolves around your personal view of yourself. When you say, "I do," you are making a vow to yourself, to God, and to your spouse. Making a vow is serious business with the Lord. This is the word of your honor. It is sacred; your character is on the line. The promise you vowed is between you and God. In the Bible, we are warned that we are not to make a vow that we are not going to stand by. Ecclesiastes 5:5 (NIV) says, "It is better not to make a vow than to make one and not fulfill it."

What does this mean? Take the vows you make very seriously. God is not playing around with you. It means that your walk with God has become amplified by adding a spouse. You are enhanced by being married. There are now two of you professing God and his love for you through his Son, Jesus Christ, together. Marriage gives the Lord a stage to demonstrate his grace and mercy to those who are the onlookers of your marriage. All marriages are heavily scrutinized and placed on a viewing stage.

This is the reason why marriages are so overwhelmingly attacked. However, it is the responsibility of the couple to always work on their marriage. What do I mean by always? Am I saying all the time? That is exactly it. You are never to stop working on your marriage. It is a commitment from sunup to sundown, twenty-four hours a day, seven days a week. The purpose of marriage is to demonstrate God's tireless love of his bride, the church. In Hebrews 13:5 (NIV), God promises, "Never will I leave you; never will I forsake you." He is with us until the end. Deuteronomy 31:6 (NIV) states we are to "be strong and courageous. Do not be afraid or terrified because of them, for the LORD your God goes with you; he will never leave you nor forsake you."

Leave No Way Out is written to help Christians remember to work on the staying power in your marriage by learning to put your marriage first.

Developing trust among you, God, and your mate should be the focus of your marriage. It is hard to remain in a marriage that is not focused on serving the Lord together as a couple. Therefore, trusting in God by cultivating a relationship with him through Jesus Christ is essential to the survival of your marriage. The other key to staying married is learning to die to oneself. An example is giving up the need to be right and turning it into a desire to become righteous. This should be emphasized in all marriages. Remember, your spouse is human. The longer you are married, the more you will learn about your partner. There are behaviors you will grow to love and admire about your mate and other character flaws you will detest and become embarrassed by.

This is when the vow "for better or worse" comes into play. Trust me: in all marriages, you will discover troubling truths about your mate, and this will be a turning point in your relationship. At this time, you might wonder if you should stay or go. That is wrong thinking. Your back door is closed, locked, and the key has been thrown out. The only reason to leave is if there's been infidelity. Matthew 5:32 (NIV) says, "But I tell you that anyone who divorces his wife, except for sexual immorality, makes her the victim of adultery, and anyone who marries a divorced woman commits adultery." That is the only time when you have a decision to make at all. All other troubles are to be taken to God in prayer first and worked out with your spouse second. This is the only way to handle the troubles that come with a marriage. Remember, God is in favor of your marriage, and he desires for it to be successful. In the next chapter, we will probe this subject more.

Finally, I ask, "Did you mean it when you said, 'I do'?" First, let's dissect "I do." This is an oath, a promise, a commitment, a vow to God. When you say, "I do," you're saying, "I can, and I am willing to be a part of this marriage." No one has forced you to say, "I do," and no one has forced you into this marriage. You are in it. So where do we go from here? Getting married is the easy part; staying married is when faith comes in. The vow is the seal. Love is not what keeps us together; it is what makes us get married. The vow is what keeps us together and forces us to sweat it out. The commitment between two people and God is the essence of the marriage; Ecclesiastes 4:12 (NIV) says, "A cord of three strands is not quickly broken." So why are Christians getting divorced at the same rate as nonbelievers?

There are two main reasons:

a) Being unequally yoked. "Do not be yoked together with unbelievers. For what do the righteous and the wickedness have in common?" (2 Corinthians 6:14 NIV); this is a command.

b) A lack of commitment to Christ and the vows that were made. "So, because you are lukewarm—neither hot nor cold—I am about to spit you out of my mouth" (Revelation 3:16 NIV).

Christians who struggle the most are either married to a lukewarm Christian or have married outside of their faith; still others have married a nonbeliever. I cannot stress this enough. This reason is the single cause of most Christian divorces. Even when two nonbelievers marry, they have a greater chance of staying together due to being equally yoked in their lack of belief.

What does this phrase mean? To be equal is to be like minded, heading in the same direction. To be yoked (blended, bonded) together means to be immersed in each other. Those who are equally yoked find it comfortable to be supportive and encouraging in their spouse's visions, hopes, and dreams. When you know a person is on the same page as you are, it eliminates most of the fighting in a marriage. It does not prevent you from arguing, but when the two of you are standing firm on the same principles, there will be less debating about how to handle normal, stressful marital issues.

The issues that plague most marriages are clearly spelled out in the Bible; it also explains how each situation is to be handled. For example, money, faithfulness, sexual morality, being committed to each other and to Christ, child-rearing; you get the point.

Note: Before you decide to get married, be sure that you are equally yoked to this person; this should not be overlooked. Divorce reveals a lack of commitment to Christ, especially when it is done out of selfish intent. Proverbs 9:10 (KJV) says, "The fear of the Lord is the beginning of wisdom." If fearing the Lord or disappointing him are not at the forefront of your mind, then you might want to reevaluate your relationship with Christ. When you became saved, you were supposed to have died to yourself and live for Christ. Galatians 2:20 (NIV) says, "I have been crucified with Christ, and I no longer live, but Christ lives in me."

The life I now live is in and through Christ. I choose to live by faith, and my marriage is one of faith. Therefore, if you feel that your happiness is more important than pleasing God, you may walk away from your committed vows. However, if pleasing the Lord is of the utmost importance to you in your walk, you will dust off your knees after praying and resume working on your marriage.

Marriage is a gift from God, but like all gifts, after you take off the wrapping paper and open the package, the anticipation is gone. After using the product, over time, years of wear and tear on the product can become apparent; your marriage may need some mending. Your marriage will require constant repairing and reinventing. Prepare yourself for a wonderful ride that will include many ups and downs, trials and tribulations; all that can be handled by God, if you let him. Remember that Philippians 4:12 (NIV) says, "I can do all things through Christ who gives me strength."

CHAPTER 2

SWEAT EQUITY

When you think of sweating, most people think of hard work. It is the main reason some people don't exercise. A fast and steady heart rate creates sweat. During this phase, when your heart is pumping at its fastest, you sweat. Sweating is wet and sticky. When I am working out, and my body begins to warm up, I become hot. I can feel my pores opening and begin sweating. The sweat continues to trickle down my face, and I instantly want to stop the workout. When you sweat during a workout, you know that you are burning fat. Knowledge of this fact is what keeps you exercising. The effort required to get to this point is why some people choose not to go to the gym. The workout alone becomes too much, and the ability to make time to get in shape can sometimes be overbearing. Making the time to work out is key to getting into shape. What you put into it is what you will get out of it. Let's look at marriage as a workout.

Have you ever complained about being tired in your marriage? Do you sometimes think about quitting, throwing in the towel, and giving up? This is why so many marriages don't make it to the first decade. Just as you do when you work out, your body begins to get weary, and you just want to stop, especially if you don't see any results. The fact that we continue to struggle with the same senseless arguments is the most frustrating part about being married. You ask yourself; When is this going to end? My husband and I will argue about pointless things, such as who should have the remote control. We often argue over disciplining the children. We've even disagreed about whether or not to call it arguing, saying we are having a passionate discussion. All I know is that we do this to the point of exhaustion. Exhaustion in a marriage will happen. You grow tired of making the same statements over and over again, or you get drained of trying to make new efforts when nothing seems to be working. At times, failure seems imminent; at this point, you want to give up and get out. Don't give up; sweat it out. Through these exhaustive moments, your marriage will get stronger.

When you walk into a gym, do you ever notice who is sweating the hardest? Look carefully; the people who are trying their hardest are usually sweating the most. There are those who appear to be in the best physical shape and seem to have barely broken a sweat. You might think that they must have been at this for years to look so good. Yet there are other people who are pounding it out on the treadmill day after day, without much to show for it. They are panting and sweating their little hearts out, doing their very best. You feel sorry for them and proud of them at the same time. To look good and stay healthy, we all must sweat it out.

Marriage is the same way. Some marriages are picture-perfect on the outside; however, on the inside, they are sweating it out. They are struggling to get through to the next day. Sounds sad, doesn't it? Even scary? But it's true. Marriage is much like preparing for a marathon. Galatians 6:9 (KJV) says, "Let us not be weary in well doing." 2 Timothy 4:7 (NIV) reminds us of the reward we are seeking, instructing us by saying, "I have fought the good fight, I have finished the race, I have kept the faith." Get the picture? Anything worth working for requires hard work, sweat, and tears.

Answer these questions:

◻ How much work are you willing to put into your marriage?
◻ Is your marriage worth sweating through the "for worse" times?

Marriage is a workout. Many people (even Christians) stop the workout before the marriage begins to form. Some days when I wake up, I don't even want to speak to my husband, let alone make breakfast for him. Nevertheless, I go into the kitchen and make a meal and serve it to him. This is because I am praying that this act of love will help me work out my animosity toward him and get me closer to reconciliation. I can only control my actions, not my husband's. My marriage is important enough for me to sweat through all things.

Think about this:

◻ Has God stopped working on you?

11

☐ Did he give up on you before you began to understand what it is he wants from you?

All God wants from you is for you to obey him, keep his commands, love your neighbor, and keep your vows. "If you love me, obey my commandments," says John 14:15 (NKJV).

Now, no one should be abused or battered. God loves us far too much to allow this to happen. We may experience pain and disappointment; however, we are never to be treated like trash. Think about what you would do if your child was sick and developed a fever. After determining how high their fever is, you would reach for some fever-reducing medication. You might need to call the doctor for additional help. Sweating it out, in this case, is not the best choice to make.

Some marriages are toxic and dangerous. If you are in a dangerous or toxic relationship, please seek help, for this could prove to be very detrimental to your health.

What do I mean by detrimental?

Another word for detrimental is harmful. Harmful relationships can lead to incarceration, child removal by social services, domestic violence, or death. Toxic relationships can be identified by major issues in your marriage, such as jealousy, a lack of security, loneliness, paranoia, and most importantly, a lack of faith in the Lord. If your life has been threatened or you are being beaten or forced to do things against your will, you should seek help and get out.

This is my second marriage, and I am sharing this with you because my first marriage was very toxic. I tried to stay for as long as I could take it; nevertheless, I might have done a disservice to my children by remaining with him for so long. Both of my daughters have anger issues; they also struggle with self-esteem and self-worth questions. Their view of marriage has been tainted, and their belief in marriage has been jeopardized because of what they witnessed. This was also true for my oldest son (who was not my ex-husband's child, but he lived in the same home with us for nine years). He started feeling like marriage was a joke and there weren't any good marriages out there anymore. I believe that when God allowed me to end my marriage, it was not for a lack of trying to keep my marriage; it was due to unfaithfulness and abuse.

I remember feeling like I was going to lose my Christianity because of my ever-growing disdain for my husband. I was beginning to hate him so much so that it scared me. I felt that my faith and that of my children were at risk, due to my lack of understanding the Bible at the time. This does not mean that you must get a divorce. What I am saying is that your life is important to God; he commands that a time for grief will come, but no one will take away your joy (John 16:22, paraphrased). It does not mean that you will not be unhappy at times during your marriage or dissatisfied with the direction of your life. However, you should never have to be afraid for your life, nor should you have to endure physical or emotional abuse.

Seeking professional help is not a sign of failure; it's a sign of commitment and strength. You help your spouse if you take the time to get yourself the help you need. Keeping your spouse's sins covered up will not bless your marriage. It is okay to share it with a professional whose job is to give you the tools you need to heal your marriage and your spouse. The choice is yours. This might include contacting the police or speaking with your pastor. In certain cases, you may need to obtain a restraining order, or you might need to leave the situation for safety purposes. You are not failing God when you are protecting yourself and your children.

What is a toxic relationship? A toxic relationship is when two people feed off each other in a negative way. They attempt to control each other through threats and strongholds. This often leads to behavior that can result in abuse, jail, or even death. In the (1993) movie *Tombstone,* A Doctor who is treating Doc Holliday; tells him, "... you need complete rest." He asks, "how are you feeling?" He replies, "better. I knew it wasn't nothing". The Doctors continues saying, "you need to quit drinking and smoking and you shouldn't be having sex." Doc Holliday's woman enters the room, he say to her, "we must talk darling. It appears that we must redefine the nature of our relationship", she feeds him a cigarette and as he pulls a drag from it. She says, "Haven't I been good to you? Aren't I a good woman?" In doing this she attempts to begin intercourse with him. He replies saying, "you're a truly good woman, and then again, you may be the Antichrist."

It's a good example of what a toxic relationship can look like. If you are no good for each other and are willing to cause harm to each other for games, not loving or protecting each other, then you are in a toxic relationship, and this too will require outside help.

I know firsthand that it is easier said than done.

Philippians 2:12–13 (NIV) says, "Continue to work out your salvation with fear [reverence or respect] and trembling, for it is God who works in you according to his will and to act according to his purpose." God does not want us to be afraid of him. He wants us to respect him to the point that we are willing to do his will out of simple obedience.

Answer these questions:

- ☐ What is God's will? His will is for you to please him.
- ☐ How can I please him? By working on your marriage all the time; this might require sweating it out through the difficult times.
- ☐ When will I know that times are difficult? Difficult times can be anything from money issues to infidelity, health issues like infertility, child-rearing, loss of a job, and dealing with an ex-spouse.

Listen to your heart. Pray to the Lord for guidance and listen to people who love you and know the Lord and respect your marriage. Be honest about the way you are feeling. Understand what it means to be safe and feel safe. Love yourself and your spouse enough to get yourself the help you need.

It is a fact that dedication and hard work produce longevity, and working together produces contentment; contentment is a primary element to remaining in the marriage. So, what is work? We all know what is required of us when we are in the workplace: commitment, dedication, showing up, keeping in contact, and good communication with our superiors. It also requires consistency, effort, trust, respect, and kindness to our coworkers. There are those who can keep a job for many years following these basic principles; however, these same people cannot remain in their marriage due to not applying themselves.

Sometimes, we can accomplish a great task by simply showing up and participating fully in the marriage. Other times, we can complete this task by remaining committed to the work ethic it takes to remain married. Marriage requires both practices. Just like with getting in shape, the first step is to show up; the next is to act.

Finally, when Jesus prayed in the garden of Gethsemane, he prayed to God and asked his Father to remove this cup from him. While praying, he was scared and trembling; he prayed so hard that he sweated blood. He knew his fate was set, but still, he had enough faith to take it to God in prayer. The night before Jesus Christ was crucified, he prayed in the garden of Gethsemane. "And being in agony, He prayed more earnestly. Then His sweat became like great drops of blood falling to the ground" (Luke 22:44 NIV). It's often hard to pray during tough situations, especially when all you want to do is leave.

Note: Your marriage belongs to God, and all marriages are work. God is the author of work, and he will never give you more than you can handle. (Read 1 Corinthians 10:13.) So handle it by handing it over to God through prayer. No one likes the effort that goes in to sweating, but we do love the outcome.

When I was preparing for this book, I spoke to ten couples who have been married for over twenty years. Now, I won't account for all ten; I'll just touch on the top three. The couple married longest has been together for over sixty-seven years and bore nine children. They both were committed to the Lord and highly involved with their church. They raised their nine children with strong Christian principles. They told me that their secret was that they were soul mates, and they were committed to staying in the marriage no matter what they endured. In the end, she went first, and he died exactly one year later; they were both in their nineties.

The second couple had been married for fifty-five years before he passed away in 2012; together, they raised nine children of their own, her son from a prior marriage, and his two daughters from his first marriage plus two more children that he had. She said that she dealt with his infidelity; by choice, she stayed. He was also an alcoholic, and this caused additional strain on the marriage. I might not agree with her choice to stay married to him and deal with his issues, but in the end, it was her choice to make.

The Bible does not say we need to get a divorce when there is infidelity; it says we can choose to stay or go. She had been married during a different era; she needed him to care for her and their children. She also loved him despite his misdeeds; in the end, this was why she chose to stay. She loves the Lord and truly believes that he has cared for her throughout their fifty-five years and had no regrets.

The third couple has been married for thirty-six years and bore six natural children, and he brought his two daughters into their marriage. They suffered from health problems and battled other issues while raising their children, such as job loss, sickness, and alcohol addiction;

even still, this couple said that when they were together, they were home, and all they wanted was to be together.

Finally, I asked the couples the same question: what is the key to a lifelong marriage? They all answered in a similar way, stating that they dealt with each situation as it came in waves. They as couples waded through the tough stuff with prayer, fear, and trembling. All the couples said that their faith in Jesus Christ and remaining in the church helped to keep their marriage focused on God's will for their lives, not their own. When one of them was down, the other spouse stepped up and held down the fort. In other words, they sweated it out together. To sum up my interviews, they had some common advice:

☐ Never remain angry for long.
☐ Remember that forgiveness is a key to salvaging all relationships.
☐ Faith is essential to the survival of your marriage.
☐ Forgive fully and for real.
☐ Do not forget to be who you really are.
☐ Have something to call your own.
☐ Live your best life, however that may look.

The death of Jesus dying on the cross for all our sins is the prime example of unconditional love and forgiveness. The key to staying married is having two people who are willing to sweat it out through the rough seasons that all marriages experience. They are to embrace the good seasons to its fullest and pray for strength through the toughest years. All marriages must go through good and bad seasons; how you choose to work through these seasons can make or break your marriage.

Ecclesiastes 3:1 (NIV) says, "For everything there is a season."

Chapter 3

Financial Equity

When thinking in financial terms, the word *equity* is defined as "a residual claimant or accrued interest" (dictionary.com); in short, value earned over time. Think about taking money and investing it. The more money you add, the more interest you will earn. This money can be used for retirement, or you can have extra money for emergencies. Knowing that you have this money set aside allows you to have financial peace. This makes you want to add even more money from every paycheck to save for the future. If you leave your money alone, it will build up equity, and later in life, you can draw from this account when you are in need. So let's look at marriage as built-up interest (equity):

- ☐ What deposits have you made in your marriage?
- ☐ Have you been making daily, monthly, or even yearly deposits?
- ☐ Are you thinking about how you can deposit more into your marriage with the same vigor you do for your money?

- ☐ How much investments have you stored up in your marriage?
- ☐ Now think of the equity you can build up with your spouse when you apply the same effort into your marriage.

Making time for your spouse is the best way to demonstrate how much you truly love them. You show love when you make daily deposits, such as making his breakfast or buying her flowers on your way home from work, cooking a romantic dinner, spending time with her or him instead of watching television or being on your computer, taking long walks or hiking, or working on a home improvement project together. Time is valuable, and you cannot get it back. Thoughtfulness and consideration build equity over time. This is when you are making great deposits into your marriage.

When times become hard, you will have earned relationship equity to make withdrawals from. The memories of the good times and time spent together make the bad times a little easier to get through. Having this reserve to draw on can be the most important asset in your marriage when your spouse has become depleted due to a bad habit, addiction, job loss, or the death of a loved one, or perhaps they are having doubts about the marriage in general.

Note: This may even happen to you; there is doubt in all marriages at some point in time. The time-equity that has been spent building your relationships is the best mental place to go to. It is there, and you can begin making withdrawals during the ugly seasons. Holding on and making withdrawals from the equity you have invested in your marriage is the greatest gift you can give to yourself. Pressing forward when all hope seems to be lost is invaluable (Philippians 3:14, paraphrased). Keeping your marriage from coming up dry is important to God.

Why do we invest? We do it so that we can have something to support us in the future.

At times, you might need to live off the accrued interest during rough times. However, during the rough season of marriage, you can remember the good times and the thoughtful moments that made you fall in love in the first place.

Consider the following:

☐ How your spouse makes you smile.
☐ Their level of intelligence.
☐ The way your spouse holds you.
☐ Their thoughtfulness for you and your extended family.
☐ If you are a blended family, you might be grateful for welcoming your children or an older parent into your home, providing for and caring for them.

These are all examples of relational deposits; over time, they are accruing lifetime interest.

Why isn't the relational investment in marriage not regarded as more valuable than money? Because we have not learned that love is more valuable than money.

When your spouse does something you feel is unforgivable, just try and remember when you did something unforgivable in the eyes of the Lord. Can you think of anything? No? That's because there is nothing you can do that God will not forgive you for (except not believe in him). This is the type of reserve thinking that can help you make it through to forgiveness.

Nevertheless, anger and disappointment are separate issues; these too can be dealt with by making withdrawals from your reserve accounts. However, as with any account, if you make too many withdrawals too often, you will deplete your funds and find yourself broke. This is when marriages become broken, and you feel like there is nowhere else to go but out. Accepting the fact that the person you love the most in the world has hurt you can be quite devastating. Moving past this hurt and disappointment is the most important part for the survival of your marriage. Let's dissect 1 Corinthians 13:4–8 (NIV). Pay close attention to verses 5 and 7. Here are some keys to surviving the disappointments that continually occur in marriages. The disappointment will change, but the way to forgive and move on will not:

"Love is patient; love is kind. It does not envy, it does not boast, it is not proud. It does not dishonor others, it is not self-seeking, it is not easily angered, it keeps no record of wrongs. Love does not delight in evil but rejoices with the truth. It always protects, always trusts, always hopes, [and] always perseveres. Love never fails."

Verse 5 talks about two powerful aspects of marriage that can be defining. It says that love does not dishonor others, and it is not self-seeking. Love is not, but we are human. What does this mean? In a marriage, you may occasionally dishonor your mate in a self-seeking manner.

Do not worry. "I am sorry" can work most of the time, but only if it comes from a sincere place.

However, we often say or do the most selfish, self-seeking acts; they cannot be covered with a simple apology. Remember that "I'm sorry" cannot cover a multitude of sins, but love will never fail. Whose love? Not yours but the love of Christ. So repent (which means to change) from your sins to the Lord and don't do it (whatever it is) again.

This leads me to verse 7: Love always protects. To love and protect is your responsibility, even in times of anger and disappointment. You are always to protect your spouse. You need to choose your words carefully and your actions even more carefully. It is not your love that will never fail, but the love that God has for you and your spouse will always remain true. This love is greater than all things in life. It is greater than fear, disappointment, or failure. His love is the love that will never fail, even when you do. It is important to always do your best to please God, all the time.

Chapter 4

Communication

It is important to know that the person you are married to is valued and cherished. Every word that comes out of your mouth toward your spouse should be considered with love and patience. Proverbs 18:21 (NIV) says, "Life and death are in the power of the tongue, and you will eat of its fruit." Although it is important to communicate both the good and the bad parts of your marriage, it is also important to consider your tone and word choice. Your spouse is not a mind reader. Never assume that he or she understands what message you are trying to convey. How are you going to make it in your marriage if you cannot trust the person you love enough to tell him or her the truth about how you truly feel?

My husband and I fight, and sometimes, it feels like it happens every day. I do try to speak kindly to him every day and not cut him down, especially in front of others. However, it does not always work; sometimes, I just let him have it, and he does me the same way. It doesn't feel good when you're on the receiving end. Nevertheless, we often sleep on it and apologize for our behavior later. Trust is the most valuable asset (outside of your relationship with Christ) to have in your marriage. Being able to speak to your spouse in an open and honest manner, no matter how vulnerable you feel, is always worth it. Having faith in your mate is the best way to stay consistent in the marriage. Communication is the next most important thing to consider.

Communication can be demonstrated in many ways. There is verbal communication; that is when you speak to each other using your words. There is also nonverbal communication; this is done through physical actions or body language. For example, using the silent treatment, not cooking for your spouse, cutting off sex, refusing to help your mate, slamming doors or leaving without telling your spouse where you are going. That kind of communication is negative, but the message is conveyed, nonetheless.

The way you speak to your spouse often depends on your mood toward them. How you choose to communicate can drive the direction of your marriage. Learning to show love through controlled communication is essential to keeping your marriage intact. Whenever two people are placed together underneath one roof, there will be contention. There must be time allotted for the two of you to form into a normal living pattern with each other.

Note: If you believe that you will never argue in your marriage, you are lying to yourself. This type of thinking can only do your marriage harm. Be realistic. Think about becoming one in marriage and what that means. Getting to know each other requires trust and communication.

Sometimes, that communication can become passionate or be demonstrated in a negative way.

Come to understand the difference between a passionate discussion and a fight. Know that physical abuse and abusive language are not good in any marriage. Arguments will happen from time to time in your relationship. You must discuss the boundaries of arguments with your spouse prior to getting married. For example, decide how you respond to an out-of-control situation or how you are going to deal with fear or feelings of betrayal. Remember that you can always agree to disagree. If you are already married, sit down with your mate and write out your agreed-upon limits. All marriages can be made new. It is never too late to start over. This is done so that you can communicate clearly but safely.

Furthermore, these agreements limit the control that either one of you has over the other. When my husband and I get into an argument, we can rely on the agreement we made prior to our marriage to help with our discrepancy. For example, we agreed that if he does not fix something that needs to be fixed within one year after I bring it to his attention, then I can use funds from our savings account to hire a professional to complete the project. We also agreed that I would discipline my four children. If he has a concern, he brings it to me in private; for example, he may want the children to do their chores correctly or follow his directions. I will address his concerns with the children and make sure they do what they are supposed to do. This doesn't always work, but it works most of the time.

Learning to Fight Fair

Marriages that are controlled by power can be demonstrated through winning arguments. Some fights are won by the person who controls the conversation. That person usually does not allow the other spouse to get a word in edgewise, or they call their spouse names or put them down. Arguments are often won by the person who holds out the longest. This might be true, but if you continue to win, and your spouse continues to lose, he or she can become bitter and resentful toward you. The bitterness then begins to grow roots. The roots are what become trees, and the trees grow leaves, and the leaves fall. So stop this plague before any roots can take hold.

How you communicate can make or break your relationship. Most importantly, you must make a commitment to **TALK**, an acronym for **Time, Attention, Love,** and **Kindness.** If you need to take some time to yourself before you talk, then take the time; however, be careful not to take too much time. The Bible says, "Do not let the sun go down while you are still angry" (Ephesians 4:26 NIV). You must find the time to make your spouse feel loved, even when he or she is not acting lovable. You are not always going to like the person you are married to. Love will never leave; it only changes in the way it feels.

Communication is the best way to keep your love strong. You must first be honest with yourself, and then you can be honest with your spouse. Keep some thoughts and feelings to yourself, especially if they are aimed to kill, steal, or destroy. Never withhold inspiration, affectionate words of love, or encouragement. Always treat your spouse the way you want to be treated. Honesty in a marriage is a catalyst to intimacy. When you know you can trust the person you are with, and be open and honest with them, then the world is at your feet. There are perks to being in sync with your mate; that is security and sex. Sex is best when the two of you are one. Once the trust has been severed, it can take years to repair. Don't let this happen, even when you feel that you cannot go on without saying something hurtful. It is better to hurt with words and ask for forgiveness than to allow lies to develop into a tear that rips a hole in your marriage. Always choose the truth and trust God. Now, there will be times when the timing of speaking the truth might need to be thought out, but the truth nonetheless will always benefit you both in the marriage. Remember, you are with this person for the rest of your life.

Can you hold a secret or keep track of your lying forever? John 8:32 (NIV) says, "You shall know the truth and the truth shall set you free."

Think about how you communicate with those you work with.

- ☐ Do you show them respect?
- ☐ Do you allow them time to finish their thoughts?
- ☐ Do you truly consider the effect that your words might have on them before you speak?
- ☐ Do you think about your word choice because you are afraid of being fired or reprimanded?

Most would say they truly take all of this into consideration before they speak to a coworker or boss.

So how much more should you consider the way you communicate with your spouse? If your spouse were your boss, would you speak to him or her this way? Well, your spouse *is* your boss. If you are truly serving God, then your spouse is to be highly respected. Your marriage is the most important earthly relationship you will ever have. You may sometimes feel as if it's the most challenging relationship you've ever endured, but it's worth it. Just as sweating it out is extremely important, talking it out is vital; the two go hand in hand.

Don't use the Bible as a tool for evil. Remember that "… the word of God is quick, and powerful, and sharper than any two-edged sword," (Hebrews 4:12, (KJV). The words that come out of your mouth cannot be taken back. You can ask for forgiveness, but once the words are out, they remain out forever. When speaking with my clients about their worst regrets, they usually say they regret the way they spoke to their loved ones. Words cannot be retracted. They cannot be erased, but they can be forgiven. The next chapter discusses the importance of forgiveness in a marriage.

Finally, what should be said when you are attempting to communicate? Great athletes must train before they compete. They train for months and years. They eat what is healthy, they drink the right juices, and they show up for practice. They study their opponent and get in shape before they step into the ring, on to a field, or on the court. They are ready to fight.

Spouses also need to get into shape and be prepared to battle, not each other, but what is to come. You are not always going to get along with your spouse, but that will never change the fact that you are married; you have to find a way to work it out. In all marriages, disagreements, arguments, or fights are going to happen. It is not that you fight or disagree, but how you prepare for your disagreement, that will make or break this conflict.

- ☐ You must be prayed up.
- ☐ Know that your love for your spouse will lead to disagreements at times.
- ☐ Prepare to not *be* right but *do* what's right.
- ☐ Allow yourself to feel your spouse's emotions and let him or her know that it's safe to openly express feelings and disappointments.
- ☐ Love him or her through disagreements, but be honest with yourself.
- ☐ Do not use harmful words toward your loved one.
- ☐ Never call your spouse a name.

Don't use names such as "stupid," "dumb," and "idiot"; curse words should never be permitted in your marriage. There is a list at the end of this book filled with words you should never use. This list begins with the above-mentioned words. Feel free to add to this list and keep it somewhere for you and your spouse to view regularly. Please take the time to add more words to this list. Pray for wisdom and reach out to your spouse when you are hurting the worst. You will not regret this decision. Remember to always apologize and ask for forgiveness; most importantly, allow yourself to be forgiven.

CHAPTER 5

FORGIVENESS

There is a time in every marriage when you come to the end of your wits and begin to struggle with your faith for your marriage. You pray and pray, but there seems to be no answer. Your heart becomes filled with rage or despair. You want to leave, and you begin looking for a way out. Your choice now is to forgive or let go. Forgiveness is a command. It is required for our salvation: "But if ye forgive not men their trespasses, neither will your Father forgive your trespasses" (Matthew 6:15 KJV). Jesus Christ died so that we can be forgiven. Nevertheless, forgiveness is a choice. It is a choice that is made when we decide that someone needs to be forgiven.

Loving your spouse is great, but it cannot always be counted on for keeping a marriage together. It can get in the way of understanding the truth that troubles your marriage. Nothing is unforgivable. However, some actions can never be forgotten. To forgive does not mean to forget. Regarding marriage, there is an inherent need for tolerance; there is also an expectation of forgiveness. If you are incapable of forgiving, then you should not consider marriage. Your spouse will do something that requires your forgiveness. Mark 11:24–25 (NIV) says, "Therefore, I tell you, whatever you ask for in prayer, believe it, and it will be yours. And when you stand praying, if you hold anything against anyone, forgive him, so that your Father in Heaven may forgive you your sins."

In other words, if you do not forgive others, then God cannot forgive you. To be forgiven requires forgiveness, and you must allow yourself to receive forgiveness from your mate; this is wisdom.

Think about this:

- □ What is it that you have done in your life that is unforgivable? According to the Bible, nothing is unforgivable (except to deny the Holy Spirit).
- □ Are there people you have not been able to forgive? Take a moment and think about it.
- □ If so, who?
- □ Why haven't you forgiven them?

If you can answer these questions, then you can begin to unlock the key to peace. Peace is a verb meaning to pacify; for example, "He offered her a peace pact." "They allowed peace to come upon them." Both examples are actions. Matthew 5:9 (NIV) says, "Blessed are the peacemakers, for they will be called children of God." It is God's desire for his children to be peacemakers. As Christians, it is imperative that we seek his peace as the only option in an impossible situation. Now this might be very difficult, but that's why we have faith. "But seek first the kingdom of God, and his righteousness; and all these things shall be added to you" (Matthew 6:33 NKJV).

Forgiveness is the first step in starting over. Forgiveness must come from the heart and be sincere. There are times when it seems that the ties just cannot be picked up and the relationship is over. It takes more than one person to complete a do-over in a marriage. After there has been great damage, or the trust has been broken, the marriage can seem to be irreparable. As said previously, the Bible states that when the unbeliever wants to go, let them go. However, if there are two believers in the home, then your choice is that the marriage needs to begin again, a do-over, if you will.

Let's start with repentance. What does it mean to truly repent? To repent is to search your heart and ask God to forgive you of your sins and to allow him to begin a new work in your life and in your marriage. To truly repent also means that you've accepted your role in the wrong or participated in the sin that's been allowed to seep into your marriage, and you've turned away from it and stopped the behavior. Revealing your faults or sins can be likened to peeling back the layers of an onion. As you begin the peeling process, tears form in your eyes, and sometimes there is burning and great pain. It hurts, and you want to stop. "No more," you say. "I cannot take the pain." So where do you go from there? You are to stand on the word of Christ and pray through the pain.

Finally, we must learn to submit to each other. Ephesians 5:21 says, "Submit to one another out of reverence for Christ" (NIV). Submission is not slavery; it is handing the reins over to the head of the home through the will of God, trusting in his word. Christ is the head of your home.

We Christians spend a lot of time resolving our issues as the world does; we go to counseling or family therapy as well as receiving acupuncture or going to the gym. We talk to our friends and often meet with others who are in similar situations. These are good options. Nevertheless, "Without faith it is impossible to please God, because anyone who comes to Him must believe that He exists and that He rewards those who earnestly seek Him" (Hebrews 11:16 NIV). In this context, you must seek God's presence and listen to him regarding your marriage. He will answer you and guide you through your troubles.

John 3:16 (NKJV) says, "For God so loved the world that he gave his only begotten Son, and whoever believes in him shall not perish but have everlasting life." God forgives us unconditionally. I am reminded of this when I hear a song by a great artist named Benny Hester; I grew up loving this song. The verse that strikes me the most is when he sings, "Then he ran to me, He took me in His arms, held my head to His chest, and said, 'My son's come home again.' 'Looked at my face, wiped the tears from my eyes, with forgiveness in His voice He said, Son, do you know I still love you?" (You can watch the video, "When God Ran," by Benny Hester on YouTube.) This is a powerful reminder that God still loves you, even if you leave him. Psalm 3 says, "Blessed are all who take refuge in him." Psalm 71:5 (ESV) says, "For you, O Lord, are my hope, my trust." God wants us to run to him with all our troubles, all our cares, and all our desires.

Note: If you are willing to wait on the Lord, He will renew your strength. I cannot promise that the situation will change, but I can assure you that when you truly seek God with your whole heart, it is you who will be changed. Know that God always has your back. This can be hard to believe at times. We need to remember to praise him, especially in the hardest of seasons. Praising God helps break strongholds and draws you closer to him. For more insight, read Psalms 9 and 20 (NIV).

LET US PRAY

Father, you are my light and my shield. With you, I shall not want. Through you, I will give you my all. Help strengthen my prayer life, in and about my marriage. Give me the willingness to seek you not only in prayer, but to seek you through your words as well. I need you, Lord, to be the head of my marriage and all it encompasses. Father, be the commander of my life.

In Jesus's name, Amen.

CHAPTER 6

REINVENTING YOURSELF

Some of you who is reading this can say, I am married now, and I feel as though a part of me is missing. The question now is, who am I? This is a question that's usually considered during the first couple of months of marriage. Questioning your role as a spouse, and the purpose of your marriage, is common. If you begin to question your life as a married person, and it consumes your thoughts, this is fear: fear of failure, fear that you made a bad decision, fear that you cannot remain in this marriage. When I married my first husband, I felt that the moment we arrived at home, he changed. It was like he flipped a switch for jealousy and insecurity, and I became under his radar all the time. Life became miserable, instantly. I had great regrets and fear. This type of fear can make you begin wondering who you are.

Women can get swallowed up in the demands of becoming a new wife. They can become confused in their new role as a wife and parent, and trying to put a home together. Men usually get lost in the providing for their family. They start working on plans for a better future.

No matter what the issues are, you can begin to feel lost or displaced within your marriage. However, it is not the marriage that is at issue; it is who you are as a person within the marriage that is in question and needs to be reinvented.

This doesn't mean that your identity as a mother or a wife is in question, but rather who are you apart from that. What have you always wanted to do with your life? Do not forget who you are.

Make goals. Where do you see yourself in one, five, or ten years?

You are the only person responsible for defining your uniqueness in your marriage.

You don't have to lose yourself when you get married. You just got married; you didn't die. You are now a wife or husband. However, you are still you. Who you were when you got married is the same person you remain after you said, "I do." Even still, you must evolve into one, with your spouse. This will take a lot of time. Be sure to speak with your spouse regarding all decisions, especially those that cost money or take you away from the home. There are some things you did when you were single that you can no longer do now that you are married. There are some things that you involved yourself in that you can no longer continue to do because you are married. No, the person you were before did not die. You've been enhanced through marriage. You are now a part of a team. It's important that you learn to play ball together and get on the same team. Still, this doesn't mean you cannot have separate interests and separate friendships. Just don't hide things or deceive each other. Share your adventures with each other. It will make you closer, and the two of you will learn more about each other. You will learn to appreciate the individual personalities you both possess, thereby making you a better you.

It is now time to reinvent yourself as a married person. For women, this can come with great difficulty, as we tend to define ourselves through our husband's identity. When I reread Genesis 3:16, I noticed that there are two parts of the punishment Eve received from God for eating the forbidden fruit. This explains to me the common bond most women share. The first verse, which we all know well, reads, "To the woman he said, 'I will make your pains in childbearing very severe; with painful labor you will give birth to children.'" It goes on to say, "Your desire will be for your husband, and he will rule over you."

There have been many explanations as to what the second curse of Eve means. Some say it is a sexual desire she will have for her husband. Few women agree with that explanation. Others believe it to mean that a woman is controlled by her husband or he rules over her and she becomes subservient to him. I believe it to be speaking to the feelings women experience once they enter a relationship. This is an overwhelming desire to have the attention and affection of her husband. Not just any random attention, but his whole devotion.

A lot of women feel the need to be the center of their husband's life. If she is not the center of his life, and this is absent, then she can become insecure; this can break loose the structure of the marriage. This is the time when insecurities are formed, and anger begins to fester, thereby creating tension and strife in the home. This is all due to having a need to be the center of his life.

If your relationship with Christ is that of trust, then the curse effect can be limited. Ephesians 5:25 (NIV) commands, "Husbands, love your wives, just as Christ loved the church." When this desire is not met by this kind of committed love, the relationship can become very strained and contentious. Most women do not recognize that they are responding to the second curse of Eve, which can create a sense of insecurity in their marriage.

When too much time is spent on blaming hormones, his job, the children, other family members, or friends for the problems in their marriage, without understanding the effects of this curse, the cycle might never end. The second curse of Eve is a topic that is not discussed often enough; it can be blamed for the demise of many relationships. What is the second curse of Eve? It could be described as insecurity, neediness and loneliness. Although these can be a real factor in your marriage, it remains to be a part of the curse.

Let's look at Ephesians 5:25–27: "Husbands, love your wives, just as Christ loved the church and gave himself up for her to make her holy, cleansing her by the washing with water through the word, and to present her to himself as a radiant church, without stain or wrinkle or any other blemish, but holy and blameless." (This is a command).

If you believe that God makes no mistakes and that he is a God of order, then you will be able to see the correlation between the two verses. God gives a woman a desire for her husband. However, God also commands a man to meet her needs in those same areas. Ephesian

6:33 (NIV) says, "However, each one of you also must love his wife as he loves himself, and the wife must respect her husband." This is needed to make it possible for the husband to follow God's expectations of him as a husband to provide his wife with God's love. Women should know that men hear love through respect; providing him with respect says to him that you love him, and he is important to you. Men should know that women hear love through attention, consideration, thoughtfulness, and time. Don't be afraid to submit to your husband because you are submitting to God. He will take care of you.

Note the following:

☐ Submission is not slavery; it is compliance and obedience to your husband's reasonable, respectful expectations.
☐ You are never to be beaten or used as a sex toy.
☐ You are never to be threatened, talked down to, hit, or made to be afraid of your spouse; this is not in God's plan for your life.
☐ Remember: let no one steal your joy (this includes your spouse).

Love and respect are two of the most incredible feelings you can experience. They are also two of the most poisonous experiences you can share. Why? How can something so wonderful also be so bad and sad? Well, in a word, faith. What does faith have to do with it? If you think about it, you get married based on faith (or you should). What does faith have to do with love and respect? Everything. If you have the faith to believe in

God and know in your heart of hearts that he is real, all knowing, ever loving, and faithful, then it is by faith and faith alone you should get married.

However, most of us today do not even consider our faith walk when we think about getting married. We think about how we feel, how our spouse treats us, and how we look together (e.g., we make a good-looking couple). Romans 5:1–2 (KJV) reads, "Therefore, having been justified by faith we have peace with God through our Lord Jesus Christ." This type of peace is the same peace all Christians should have in their marriage, because it comes from the Lord, not from humans.

Your faith is not in your spouse but rather in Jesus, who lives in him or her. When you are going through hard times in your marriage, you should talk, pray together, and pray alone. For more information, read Philippians 4:6. You should never punish your spouse, ever (this is evil and brings strife into your marriage). Forgiveness is a powerful part of marriage. It acts as a sedative for both partners and is music to our Father's ears. He loves a peacemaker. Matthew 5:9 (KJV) says, "Blessed are the peacemakers, for they will be called children of God." Remember, if you are married and are equally yoked as a Christian, your spouse can be humbled through your prayers. However, if you are in the wrong, then be prepared to be humbled. Humility is a gift. It demonstrates that your walk with God is solidified. It shows that you not only know him, but you also seek him. You understand that he is the Lord of your life. Husbands should pray over and for their wives, and likewise, wives should pray for their husbands, daily.

Most people dedicate their lives to their job. If you ask someone what their name is, most people will answer you and add their occupation as well. It is like people need to justify that they are somebody. Their occupation is how most people view themselves. Some people most often describe themselves by how they make a living, instead of how they are living. People who are unemployed or disabled, or stay-at-home mothers, may identify themselves as such. Your job is not who you are; it is what you do. Describing your work first, instead of mentioning your family or the Lord, speaks volumes as to what matters. It says a lot about the priorities in your life.

I believe myself to be a hardworking, Christ-dedicated person. However, I know that I may seem self-serving and lazy at times. I am also bull-headed and can be self-righteous. But I have always loved people and wish to do good, not harm.

Knowing who you are is a very important step in understanding who you are as a husband or wife. Being able to define yourself as the person you are instead of what you do will keep your mind focused on your Christ-walk, your marriage and your family.

Think about this:

- ☐ What is your title?
- ☐ Who do you say you are?
- ☐ How would others describe you?
- ☐ Who truly knows the real you?

As a married woman, we first accept our new identity as Mrs. _____. Then we make it final by applying to the Social Security office for a new card. We get a new driver's license, and then we officially change the names on our bank accounts. Finally, we change our name at the workplace. This is a very arduous task for a woman. Men do not have to do any of this. However, women choose this task to take on when they say, "I do." The new identity can become a metaphor for how a woman begins to feel when she chooses to get married. But these same steps can cause a woman to feel as though she has lost herself. It can depend on how well the marriage is going as to how long it will take for a woman to feel this way. If the marriage is good, then it takes her more time to begin longing for her personal identity, apart from her husband.

If the marriage is going bad or she is lonely, then the yearning can come quicker. That woman can begin to feel as though she is lost and cannot find herself. This can show itself through different signs, such as overeating, indulging in a lavish lifestyle, or changing her hair style. She might even want to have a baby. Feelings of a loss identity can be demonstrated by constant whining or having crying fits.

Trying to rediscover yourself within a marriage can be difficult if you don't include your spouse in the thought process; at least then, you know you already have their support. No, you are not asking permission; you are sharing your desires and your dreams with your life-mate. If this is true love, your mate will want to reach out to help see your desire become a realization. That is why I wrote this book. My husband and kids helped to build me an office where I can write. My husband also periodically checks in on me to see how it's going. That's love.

When I wanted to lose weight, I discussed it with him, and we agreed that I would join a gym. Now I have one in my home. He wants to ski and play in a pool tournament, so I am making sure that happens for him. Now, his desires cost money, as did building my writer's room. However, due to his desires being an ongoing financial obligation, we must take it one month at a time. Nevertheless, we never stopped planning. There have been many arguments, and the blame has been passed to each other during the projects. However, forgiveness works over time, and we were able to push through our disagreements and sweat it out. In addition, we built up a lot of equity to be considered during future disagreements.

Discovering your passion or desire can be tricky when you are inundated with the rigors of life. Nevertheless, you can rediscover your passions by trying different activities or skills, such as going back to school or getting a job. There are cooking, yoga, and karate classes to consider.

When the search for self is turned on, bitterness and frustration can seep into your marriage. It is very important that you discuss your feelings with your spouse. When in doubt, reach out and reach up. You can often find renewed strength in the Bible, Christian music, and spiritual help books. You can also reach out to an uplifting friend, someone who has proven to be reliable, who is encouraging, and who will stand with you as well as pray for you. Be sure your friend is in support of marriage, and remember to pray always.

CHAPTER 7

COMMITTED TO GOD

There may come a time in your marriage when you say, "Enough is enough." You've given your all, and all you have left to hold onto is the commitment you made. At times, this commitment was all I could grab ahold of to help me remain in my marriage. There have been many tough times throughout my marriage when I wanted out, especially when my son, Tomas, passed away. I wanted nothing and no one. It was at that time when my commitment to God and the vows I made were the only things that kept me from running to the hills (metaphorically speaking); all I could remember was my love of God through Jesus Christ, my Savior, and how this would not be pleasing to him.

I am married because I love my husband, but what makes me stay married is my desire to please God. I want to make him proud of me. I want to hear him say, "Well done, good and faithful servant" (Matthew 25:23 NIV). I desire to be right in his eyes, although I fail more often than I succeed. When I am unable to walk to him, if my heart is pointed toward Jesus, he will always pick me up and celebrate my return. 1 Thessalonians 2:4 (NIV) says, "But just as we have been approved by God to be entrusted with the gospel, so we speak, not to please man, but to please God who tests our hearts."

Ask yourself these questions:

☐ Is your relationship with the Lord almighty the most important relationship in your life?
☐ Are you committed to God?

Are you committed to your marriage?

Proverbs 3:5–6 (EVS) says, "Trust in the Lord, with all your heart, and do not lean on your own understanding, in all your ways acknowledge him, and he will make straight your paths." When you are committed to God, you are crying out for his guidance. Your will is to please him. Your daily walk should be about learning to lean on him and trust his ways. "Your ways are not my ways says the Lord" (Isaiah 55:8 NIV). Understanding his will for your life requires listening skills and learning how to live and walk by faith. "For we walk by faith not by sight" (2 Corinthians 5:7 NIV).

In the spring of 2014, I lost my oldest child. Tomas was twenty-four years old. He was a beautiful young man whom I love and adore. I miss him more than words can say. Like my son lived his life, I have also been committed to God for a very long time. My commitment to the Lord has kept me from going off the deep end during my period of grief. Grieving Tomas's death has been so hard and intense that nothing else matters to me. My marriage suffered after the death of my son, due to our different grieving methods. I know that my husband loved Tomas very much, but his relationship, being his stepfather, was different from mine. His grieving and healing was much quicker than mine.

After Tomas's death, the candle that had been lit in my heart at the time of his conception was blown out. This left me with a Tomas-size hole in my heart. A piece of me has died. This hole can only be filled with the love of God, through Jesus Christ. I cannot begin to describe the pain and despair I feel. I wanted to give up on everything in my life, including my marriage. This is not only when the vows I've taken come into consideration, but when the trust I've developed in the Lord, by walking my faith out, becomes most vital.

I never understood what true love was until my first child was born. Once Tomas was placed in my arms, my heart was filled with a love that was indescribable. That was when I began to understand what unconditional love is and how it was possible to love someone instantly. As far as I knew, Tomas was going to be in my life forever. I was committed to caring for him for the rest of his life. I vowed to protect him, love him, and forgive him without reservation.

I believe that when you become a parent for the first time, you understand what true love is. However, the commitment is not automatic for some; you'd think that it would be, but it isn't. I know that being a parent is the most wonderful calling and the hardest a person can ever have. It requires love, selflessness, dedication, and commitment. The love parents have for their children is almost instantaneous. However, this is not so for the love between two people; that may require more time for love to develop and for trust to ensue. It will get stronger if you let it. This too requires love, selflessness, dedication, and commitment.

I ask these questions:

- ☐ Are you committed to God and to your spouse?
- ☐ Are you committed to God enough to remain with your spouse?

Ecclesiastics 4:12 (KJV) says, "And if one prevails against him, two shall withstand him, and a three-fold cord is not quickly broken." It is possible to marry someone you like a lot, and thought you loved, only to discover later that the two of you do not love each other.

What do you do now? Think about this: you are married. Leave no way out.

- ☐ Deal with it.
- ☐ Work it out.
- ☐ Do not lose hope.

Remember that "with God all things are possible to those who love him according to his will and purpose" (Matthew 19:26 NIV).

Think about your relationship.

- ☐ Are you as committed to the marriage as you are to be a parent or to your job?
- ☐ Are you committed to the point that you would not quit on your marriage, as if your spouse were your child?

If your answer is no, and you are not married, then you should reconsider your decision to marry. However, if you are married, but you are not as committed to your spouse as you should be, then it is time for you to reevaluate your commitment to your marriage and seek help. Remember, divorce is reserved for infidelity only, and even then, it is a choice.

When I got married for the first time, I left a back door open in my heart, believing that I could always get a divorce if things did not work out.

When I stood in the courthouse, the judge asked me, "Do you take this man to be your lawful, wedded husband?"

I froze. I did not answer him because my heart told me to say no.

The judge asked me for a second time, and I replied, "I guess."

The next thing I knew, I was married to a man I no longer loved or even liked. My back door was wide open, and after years of problems and abuse, I got my escape due to infidelity, and we were able to get a divorce.

The marriage was over, and I was left with three children to provide for. This was not God's plan for my life, nor was it his image of what marriage should be. I not only married a man I was unevenly yoked to, but I also married against God's will.

These are my questions for you:

- ☐ Are you committed to Christ?
- ☐ Is your walk with God ready for the battles of marriage?

- ☐ Have you gotten prayed up?
- ☐ Do you have a prayer partner who is in favor of your marriage?
- ☐ Do you know what God wants for you?

In Matthew 7:7–8 (NIV), we are encouraged to "ask and it will be given to you; seek and you will find; knock and the door will be opened to you. For everyone who asks receives; the one who seeks finds; and to the one who knocks, the door will be opened."

Philippians 4:6 (NLV) says, "Don't worry about anything; instead, pray about everything. Tell God what you need and thank him for all he has done." Sometimes, he says yes, and other times, he says no. There will be times when he says nothing at all because you already know the answer. In those times, you are to do nothing and let go and let God.

So how can you do all of this? Psalm 37:4 says that we are to "take delight in the LORD, and he will give you the desires of your heart." If you are truly committed to a relationship with God, and you believe that Jesus died on the cross for you and your spouse, then you know that God is in favor of your marriage, and he wants it to succeed. He would like for you to be true in him and his perfect will for your life. Please allow him to direct your path.

Commitment requires devotion, dedication, supplication, and lots of prayer. God trusts you to trust him to do the right thing in your life. Do you believe that his ways are not our ways, but they are the way he wants you to go? Walk with him, spend time with him, and give every problem to him. Give God your marriage, and let him decide what is right for you. Remember, when you are getting married, you must leave no way out.

LET US PRAY

Lord, protect and guide me as we walk through this journey in life. We as a couple have chosen to be with each other, as we have chosen to be committed to you. We are lifers. However, our hearts at times make us feel as if we have a decision to make concerning our commitment to this marriage. Lord, be the Lord of this marriage and remain in our midst. Your word says a strand of three cords is not easily broken. Make the bond between the two of us stronger than ever. Mark 10:9 (KJV) says, "What therefore God hath joined together, let not man put asunder." I claim this for my marriage and all marriages.

In Jesus's name, Amen.

CHAPTER 8

UNDERSTANDING

When you talk about understanding one another, you must know that your communication is not only audible but external. As you grow together, you develop a kind of telepathic connection. You begin to anticipate each other's needs. As a woman, you grow and learn how to meet your husband's tangible needs, such as feeding him, having sex with him, or learning how he likes to be pleasured. You learn how to soothe your spouse in his or her hour of need. You also learn when you should back off and allow your spouse room to breathe. Give him or her space and time.

As husbands, you learn to anticipate when you are aggravating your wife. Understanding this helps you learn to know when you should back off and give her time. You are also teaching this to your children, as well as other people who might be observing your marriage. By providing her with time and not invading her space, that in a sense is showing love. You also will learn how to anticipate her sexual needs. When you take the time to feed her and care for her when she is not feeling well, that is a great act of compassion. It shows that you are devoted to her and you truly care. This type of knowledge doesn't happen overnight. It takes lots of time to develop.

This is what the Bible means by growing together and becoming one. In a sense, this is a part of the process of becoming one person: sensing each other's needs ahead of time. Much like God did to the people of Israel when he provided them manna from heaven, or when he allowed the Israelites to get a king, when God really did not want them to have a king. Yet because they wanted one, he provided one for them. He provided for the needs of his people out of love. God stepped out of his comfort zone for those he loved. All this, because he was trying to meet their needs, and much like the people of Israel, we are often ungrateful. Learn to be grateful to your mate and provide for his or her needs out of love. Step out of your comfort zone and demonstrate unconditional love. He or she will appreciate you more for it.

In our ungratefulness toward one another, husbands and wives begin to complain about the things that we do for each other. Instead of learning to be grateful that we have one another, we often take advantage of the kindness of one another. We turn that kindness into areas of complaining and grumbling. We tend to forget that what we are receiving from our spouse is love. Instead, we feel that they aren't giving us their best. The heart becomes selfish; we forget that the needs that are being met are selfish inhibitions. Yet when our husband or wife does not give us what we want, when we want it, or the way we want it, we become like bratty children who are pouting in a store because our parents didn't buy us a toy.

We begin to sound like spoiled children on Christmas Day who only received four gifts, instead of fourteen gifts. We become ungrateful and act out in a way that is unflattering; if this is done in front of others, then you are harming your spouse. Becoming one is a job. It is hard work. It takes many years of hard work, sweat, coupled with great communication, love, trust, and lots of forgiveness to make your marriage real. It is a combination of all the subjects we have covered in this book.

If we do not learn to sacrifice for one another and give in to each other to meet the needs of the person we love, then what we do is in vain. When I met my husband, I learned very quickly that he and his family were not into giving gifts. I, on the other hand, come from a long line of gift-givers. We give for holidays and for birthdays. We are a very celebratory family, whereas my husband's family rarely meet for any gatherings.

When we first met, I invited his siblings from out of town and family from all around to come out to celebrate his birthday together. They did come out and enjoyed the day with him. However, I was very angry with him because he didn't appreciate it. He said it was very unnecessary, and he would rather have the money I spent on the party. I was heartbroken and turned off by his lack of unappreciation for my gift. It took me many years to realize that he would rather have food than a gift. He sees love through his stomach. If you cook him a great meal and make it just for him, he thinks you love him more than anyone in the world. I, on the other hand, would prefer an audacious gift. I don't need a trip to France, but I would like to have tickets to *Hamilton* and maybe a night out on the town in a fancy dress. He's learning that I see love through thoughtful actions. I've learned throughout the years that he feels love by way of respect and food. Although he appears to be simple, he is complicated.

In 2012, I had a hysterectomy. My husband did not understand why I was unable to cook for him. So he picked up the phone, called my mother, and said that I was not feeding him. Oh, how furious that made me. I was so angry that I could have used foul language toward him for months. However, I chose to ignore him. I was sick, and I could not cook; therefore, I had purchased easy-to-cook items, such as food that could be placed in the microwave and heated. I even made crockpot meals prior to my surgery. In addition, I bought bunches of Ramen noodles for him and the children. He had to learn over the years that I am not a short-order cook; I am his wife. As I've had to learn to cut down on his expectations of me, he has learned to ramp up my expectations of him.

When Christmas comes and I don't receive a gift, or when our anniversary passes by and he doesn't mention it, not even a card, I get angry and hurt and feel unloved. We both have had to work at the areas where we are weakest in our lives. I understand that my husband was married to a Jehovah's Witness; they did not celebrate birthdays or any holidays. So for many years, he did not have to think about purchasing gifts or remembering holidays, not even for his children's birthdays. Now he is married to me, a person who loves to celebrate everything just because I love to celebrate life. I also love to cook, give gifts, and spoil my husband. However, since Tomas has passed away, those days have dissipated from my heart, and I have had to learn how to conjure them up again in a different way. I need to remember that it takes two to be active participants in a marriage for it to work. It is important for me to remember that I have a marriage to work on always, all the time, twenty-four hours a day, seven days a week.

Remembering my duties as a wife and the vows I made to God gives me the strength to push through to another section of my life that I might not want to be a part of. After you lose a child, there is nothing in the world that can compare. However, in the book of Jeremiah, it reminds us that the two greatest losses a person can endure is the loss of a child and the loss of a spouse. At this time in my life, I cannot imagine my husband not being here. Despite all the problems we have gone through, the good times and the bad times, in sickness and in health, for richer and for poor, we have survived. Imagining life without him in it is unbearable and even a bit scary.

My husband and I are not perfect, nor do I expect any marriage to be perfect. But when people come to me and say they cannot do their marriage any more, I do expect to hear that they have worked on it as hard as they can and that they have given it over to God. You should never even consider separating unless there is abuse or infidelity. Divorce does not always have to be the option.

I have a good man, a very good husband. He is a loving, caring, kind, sacrificing husband. Yet at the same time, with all the doting I do all over him, he can be very selfish. At times, he thinks only of himself and me meeting his needs. He can also become an extreme complainer when he wants to be. He can be stubborn.

He does not listen well and feels that I am the one who must have my way. He says that if I don't, then I would choose not to do the cooking. He could be right. However, I clean for myself. I don't want my house dirty; it drives me crazy. There are times where I have done spiteful things. I have washed only my clothes and left his there purposely, because I was angry with him. I have cooked a meal for me and the kids and left him to get some Ramen noodles. These things may sound very cold-hearted and un-Christian, but we are being real here.

Marriage is not about being perfect; it's about two human beings who love each other and are trying to work out their lives together. If you are blessed, as I know you are, then you can work out your marriage together, living with another person who you like and get to have sex with, without guilt or fear of judgment. This is living abundantly.

Throughout history, marriage has not always been a perfect union. Some couples come together, and it is natural. They love each other instantly, like Isaac and Rebekah. (You can find their story in Genesis 24.) He went into the tent, made love to her, and thereby they were married. Don't we wish it was always that simple? Well, it's not. Maybe it could be, if we wanted to let someone else pick out our mate. Prayerfully, we will love that person instantly and make many babies together and live on, until God calls us home. However, sadly, we live in a world of internet dating and conjugal hookups, but it happens in the Christian world as well, and we are lonelier than ever. It takes longer to find someone we want to be with. By the time we find that person, we have lived half of our lives alone. Today, you see more older parents who have a brand-new baby, and in my head, I'm thinking, *Thank you, Holy Father, that my children are all grown.* I have grandkids now, so when I see another person who is the same age as I am, and they are just beginning their family, I pray for them. I was tired at the age of twenty-six, when my last child was born. I pray for their strength. Now, I am not knocking what they do or why they do it. I think it is great that they took the time to make a family. All I am saying is people are waiting for perfection in a spouse, and that type of selfishness sure does take a toll on our years. It makes our lives a lot harder than they need to be. The new generation is paying for it by putting off beginning a family until later in life.

What I love about my life with my husband is that we spend it together serving the Lord. We may not be perfect in our service to the Lord, but we try to do the best we can to exemplify his graciousness in our lives. Together, we have seven kids. In addition to the kids, we also have a daughter-in-law, who is gorgeous and sweet. We have two grandchildren who are loved and adored, and finally, we have three dogs. They drive my husband crazy, but they bring richness to our lives every day. I've been blessed abundantly with love, companionship, and joy, but we've also suffered through great sorrow and pain. As I write this book, I do it with tears in my eyes and joy in my heart.

"In sickness and in health" is a very real part of growing together and becoming one. In 2008, before we got married, my husband was diagnosed with prostate cancer; soon after, in 2009, Tomas had to have brain surgery to help combat his epilepsy. In that same year, my husband had his prostate cancer surgery removal, which left him with a 5 percent chance of it reoccurring.

Prior to our engagement, while dating, he struggled with his fidelity, and he didn't know if he really wanted to be with a woman with four children. I struggled with our fourteen-year age difference. I didn't know if I wanted to be with a man who was that much older than me. We struggled during those first years. In those two and a half years of courtship, he underwent a complicated heart surgery to repair an aortic valve replacement; he also had mitral valve repair and suffered from cardiomegaly. You see, he was born with a hole in his heart; it was fixed in 1964, but years later, it came back in a big way. A month prior to his surgery, I underwent surgery on my knee to repair my ACL (anterior cruciate ligament), and went through six weeks of recovery, followed by physical therapy. It was during that time that he proposed marriage to me. We went through classes for marriage preparation and for blended families. We found both classes to be very helpful.

Yet still, applying those skills and advice after you get married can be nearly impossible. Although we both attended the same classes, we received different messages. It was only two months into our marriage when we found ourselves in therapy with our pastor at the church. It was like I was going through some sort of buyer's remorse, like after you buy a car and drive it off the lot, you think, *What have I done?* Although I never regretted marrying my husband, I did experience a sort of remorse for the loss of my independence. It didn't mean I didn't love him or that I regretted getting married. It meant that I was scared. I wasn't sure if I knew him the way I thought I should when I said, "I do."

This is another reason I wrote this book: to remind you of your commitment. Once you say, "I do," leave no way out. Although scared, I knew that my doors were shut and that I had made a promise to God and everyone, that I do, and will forever, until death. I was left with no other option than to sweat it out, and develop equity, and make withdrawals from our love bank when needed. After all, God is the one.

CHAPTER 9

ABOUT JEALOUSY

If you want to kill your marriage quickly, you can do this by reacting one way: with jealousy. Proverbs 27:4 (NIV) says, "Anger is cruel and fury overwhelming, but who can stand before jealousy?" This is what the Lord says. 1 Corinthians 3:3 (NIV) says, "You are still worldly for since there is jealousy and quarreling among you, are you not worldly? Or are you not acting like mere humans?" Early in the book, I wrote that as Christians, we are to act differently, think differently, react differently, and behave differently; that is because we are different.

When it comes to having a jealous spirit, this is an evil spirit; it's a demonic possession. We need to swiftly cast it out of our lives and back into the hands of the Lord. Jealousy will kill the essence that was in your marriage. The spark that was in your eyes and your love for him or her will die because of the lack of trust.

The root of jealousy is lack of contentment. It's a sign of insecurity. Some say it's a sign that you are doing something wrong in your life, so therefore, your mate must also be doing the same thing. However, if you spend most of your marriage looking to see if your spouse is cheating on you or doing something wrong, you're wasting your time. The Bible says, "You may be sure that your sin will find you out" (Numbers 32:23 NIV). So if there's something you're doing that's wrong, be careful because the Lord will reveal it, somehow, someway.

Be honest in your marriage; this is the best advice anyone can give. Love the person you are with. 1 Corinthians 10:13 (NIV) says, "No temptation has overtaken you except what is common to man. And God is faithful: he will not let you be tempted beyond what you can bear. But when you are tempted, he will also provide a way out so that you can endure it."

Whenever you decide that you might not be able to withstand the temptation coming from another human being, cast that to God immediately and get yourself out of that situation. Run, run, run as fast as you can. Don't let the devil, who comes to kill, steal, and destroy your marriage, have a foothold. Cast him back into the pit of hell, where he lives. Nonetheless, it is up to you. You need to make this choice. You must decide that your marriage is worth saving. As I said earlier, speaking from 1 Corinthians 13:4 (NIV) "Love is patient, love is kind. It does not envy, it does not boast, it is not proud." In marriage, you will fight, and you will have disagreements throughout your married life. Don't make that the heart of your marriage. Your life means more to God than anything. Your happiness and your contentment are to be rested in the arms of the Lord.

When you rely on God to be your Savior and put him in control of your marriage, you will learn that there is no need to worry. He has all of this in his hands. "And I saw that all toils and all achievements spring from one person's envy of another. This too is meaningless, a chasing after the wind" (Ecclesiastes 4:4 NIV). There is no need for us to be chasing after the wind. A person either wants you or doesn't. So don't run merely for the sake of chasing a person; God says that if they want to go, let them go (paraphrased from 1 Corinthians 7:15). Your heart belongs to the Lord, and your life is his. Keep your eyes to the Lord. "Don't speak evil against each other, dear brothers and sisters. If you criticize and judge each other, then you are criticizing and judging God's law. But your job is to obey the law, not to judge whether it applies to you" (James 4:11 NLT).

Remember that you *are* your brother's keeper, but the Lord is the judge and jury. Whatever you do not see, or whatever you do not know, don't concern yourself with it; it doesn't matter if it doesn't harm you. Let God be God; let him be the ruler of your life, the constructor and author of your world.

Finally, I add this nugget of wisdom from Proverbs 14:30 (NLT), which says, "A peaceful heart leads to a healthy body; jealousy is like cancer in the bones." Don't let jealousy into your heart. If it's already there, begin to pray immediately, "Lord, remove this from me. Give me peace and provide me with a world of contentment." If your husband or wife is cheating, it's time for you to pray for God to reveal whether you should stay or go. "Then you will know the truth, and the truth will set you free" (John 18:32 NIV). Go, and be with God.

Chapter 10

Conclusion

Marriage is not as complicated as we make it out to be. It's quite easy. You decide to get married to someone you believe you love and intend on loving for the rest of your life, even though it's a mystery. All marriages have a 50-50 chance of making it. There are two people who each make one part of the 50 percent. Your level of commitment is key. If you are both equally committed to the marriage, it will work; we cannot stop normal things from happening. Deaths will happen in families. Addictions will happen. Verbal abuse or even physical abuse might happen (even though it should not). However, ask any two people who've been married for a period of time, and they will say they've experienced something unexpected during their marriage.

When you watch a soap opera, you see characters falling in love, but have you ever considered how often they get divorced and remarried? This happens repeatedly, sometimes to the same person. It doesn't matter if it's their brother-in-law or their father's best friend. Oh, it's so Hollywood. However, in real life, it's much simpler than that. You will marry, or you won't; this is the cut-and-dried truth of marriage. The question is, why are you getting married? Are you getting married because someone is telling you to? This is for the rest of your life.

The apostle Paul said it was better to stay single, like him (1 Corinthians 7:8). He said he served the Lord freely, with no ties, and had no family. I say if you are single, you are still married because you're already married to the Lord. However, in truth, God tells us we can get married. He has sanctioned love for life. So many people enter their marriage, believing they are going to be totally true. When you get married, that person becomes yours, and you become that person's. That is okay; that's what it means when you grow and become one. However, becoming one doesn't mean you're on an island of your own or you cannot be your own person. All it means is that you're a part of a team. I would definitely advise people who are thinking of getting married to keep being who they are; keep a journal before you get married about the things you love now, because children will change your relationship; they will change you. Time will change your relationship; it will change you. Hurts, sicknesses, job losses, financial troubles, and the death of certain people will change you. In order for you to maintain the person you are today and obtain some of those dreams that you still desire, depend on God. You may not be able to reach all of those dreams, but God will make a way. He wants us to live the abundant life (John 10:10). He wants us to have a meaningful and bountiful life.

There is nothing for us to be ashamed about if we are living a good life. However, we are the biggest hindrance in our achievement of ushering in our goals. I once was married to someone who stifled my dreams. I didn't know before we got married, but my ex-husband didn't want me to go to school. He didn't want me to achieve more out of my education. For the first few years of my adult life, I was at home with my children. Don't get me wrong; I loved it. However, I was stifled out of obtaining my education because he prohibited it. He didn't allow it, and he threatened me at times. He locked me in the house, so I could not go anywhere, and he would take the phone from the house to work with him. In those days, I thought I was being an obedient and good wife. It was his paranoia or lack of confidence in himself that interfered with our marriage. My inability to reach out and become the person I wanted to be, this made me bitter and amongst other things, it killed our marriage.

I didn't realize I had been stifled until I divorced him and went to school to obtain my degree. I relearned what is was I wanted to become. I rediscovered the artist in me and became it. In my marriage now, I have a very loving husband who is supportive and encourages me to spend time doing the things I want to do. I also encourage him to step out in faith and do the things that he likes.

All I'm saying is, be careful not to lose who you are in your relationship. You are still two individual people. You have individual likes and dislikes. You have individual desires and individual dreams. You also have collective dreams and desires. You are to live out these collective dreams and desires together as one. However, you should very much remain as an individual who is becoming one.

You need to walk out your hopes and dreams with

the support of your mate. You need their support so that you can reach the stars without conflict. If you do this, you will be able to live the life that God intends for you to live. Not all of us are called to be Nobel Prize-winning poets or the president of the United States. Some of us are called to be homemakers, teachers, doctors, and lawyers. Still others are called to become welders or construction workers. These are all noble positions where we are all able to help someone and make someone's life good. Do not be discouraged in trying your dream and failing at it; if problems arise in your life, things will settle down again. When I began to write this book, I had all four children, but during the last chapter of this book, I lost my oldest son. I couldn't keep writing. Look, here I am now, three and a half years later, completing this book for publication.

Life got in the way, but life also reminded me that I have dreams and desires. I have a job to do for God. I believe that writing this book is part of my job. It's what I need to do for the Lord. Marriage and life are gifts. Let no one steal it from you, not even your spouse. If your marriage needs a break, then take one; you must be faithful and know that you can trust God.

This book was written in hopes that you will consider marriage honestly, truthfully, and from your heart. I pray that you will not take it lightly when deciding whether you should or should not say, "I do." And if you've already said, "I do," it's important that you learn to sweat out the troubled times; use your equity through the troubled seasons. Learn to make sensible withdrawals from the equity that you've put into your marriage, but try not to deplete it by being needy or greedy. You both need to try to outdo each other with the contributions you make into your marriage.

Most importantly, communicate with your words and not your body language. Be careful not to shut out your loved ones; the person you married is the most important person in your life. He or she is the one who will be with you after the kids have left and after the grandkids are off. Your spouse will be there. This is your reward; you will have a lifetime to share with the person of your dreams.

Most importantly, don't lose the trust of the one you love; if that happens, do whatever you can, at all cost, to get it back. Forgive if you can. Remember that toxicity in a marriage or relationship is not of God. Do whatever you can to flee from it. Do whatever you can to get rid of it. Be conscious that you're not just leaving a relationship that is hard or stressful; rather, you know you are fleeing from a truly abusive relationship. You will know this through the voice of God in his wisdom. Receive counsel from a professional who is in that field, not from your girlfriend who's never been married, or your mom who's been married five times.

Find friends who love the Lord, a friend who will pray with you and fast with you. These are the people you want to seek counsel from.

Remember, you do not have to get a divorce; you can take a timeout, a break, if you agree (sometimes even if you don't). If you need to, you can leave for a while; you can go somewhere and take a break from each other and weigh out everything, with fear and trembling. Give it to God and decide later. The world is watching your marriage, and the world views God through your marriage. We are examples of the one and only living Christ; therefore, we must be very careful with the decisions and choices we make.

Do not get into marriage haphazardly. If you are hesitant, there is time; if he or she finds someone else, or something in life happens, then that was not meant to be. Accept it and move on. Do not force a bad situation. It is like trying to push a square peg into a round hole; the force will tear it apart. If you have children, be careful of whatever decisions you make, in and out of the marriage; they will always remember what they've seen. Children learn from their parents. Most importantly, if you do decide that this marriage isn't for you and there are children involved, don't bring your children into the ugliness that is a divorce.

A divorce is the death of a family. Please consider it with everything that is in you before you make that decision. James 5:3 (NIV) says, "The root of all strife is selfishness." Look inside yourself deeply; make sure that you are not being selfish when you make the decision to leave your marriage. Make sure that you are not the cause of the divorce; if you are, then you need to get down on your knees and ask for forgiveness; beg for forgiveness from any stain on your marriage. Get rid of it. You can do it with these three things:

1. Say, "Get thee behind me, Satan! You are a stumbling black to me;" (Matthew 16:23 NIV).
2. "...I can do all thing through Christ who strengthens me!" (Philippians 4:13 NLT).

3. Cast(ing) all your cares on him, because he care(th) for you (1 Peter 5:7 KJV).

Say it. Believe it. Read it. Live it. Now walk it out. Blessings to you all.

A Final Prayer

Father, I ask that for those who've taken the time to read this book, you give them the strength to stay the course of their marriage and to sweat out the tough times. Allow them to ask you for guidance, direction, and strength in all things, always. Give them the ability to remain steadfast and diligent, never giving up hope. Protect their marriage and renew it by your strength, in Jesus's name. Amen.

NEVER USE WORDS (N.U.W)

When angry, it's hard to choose your words carefully; nevertheless, you must remember that your words cannot be retracted. Be aware who you're speaking to. This is the person you love and made a vow to. Never use curse words, especially toward each other.

James 3:9 (NIV) says, "With the tongue we praise our Lord and Father, and with it we curse human beings, who have been made in God's likeness."

Feel free to add your own words to this list:

1. Stupid
2. Dumb (or dummy).
3. I hate you.
4. Divorce.
5. Idiot.
6. I don't love you anymore.
7. You're no good.
8. I never loved you.
9. You're not loved.

Appendix

Scripture References

When You Say, "I Do," Do I Really?

1 Corinthians 7:15 (NLT)

1 Thessalonians 5:17 (KJV)

2 Timothy 2:15 (ASV)

Genesis 2:24 (NIV)

Genesis 2:41 (NIV)

Ecclesiastes 5:5 (NIV)

Hebrews 13:5 (NIV)

Deuteronomy 31:62 (NIV)

Matthew 5:32 (NIV)

Ecclesiastes 4:12 (NIV)

2 Corinthians 6:14 (NIV)

Revelation 3:16 (NIV)

Proverbs 9:10 (KJV)

Galatians 2:20 (NIV)

Philippians 4:12 (NIV)

Sweat Equity

John 14:15 (NKJV)

John 16:22 paraphrased

Philippians 2:13 (NIV)

John 14:15 (NKJV)

Luke 22:44 (NIV)

1 Corinthians 10:13 (NIV)

Genesis 2:18 (NIV)

Ecclesiastes 3:1 (NIV)

Philippians 3:14 (paraphrased)

1 Corinthians 13:4–8 (NIV)

Hebrews 11:16 (NIV)

Reinventing Yourself

Genesis 3:16 (NIV)

Ephesians 5:25 (NIV)

Romans 5:1–2 (KJV)

Committed to God

Matthew 25:23 (NIV)

1 Thessalonians 2:4 (NIV)

Isaiah 55:8 (NIV)

2 Corinthians 5:7 (NIV)

Ecclesiastics 4:12 (KJV)

Matthew 19:26 (NIV)

Matthew 7:7 (NIV)

Philippians 4:6 (NLV)

Psalm 37:4 (NIV)

Communication

Proverbs 18:21(NIV)

Hebrews 4:12 (KJV)

Forgiveness

Matthew 6:15 (KJV)

Mark 11:24–25 (NIV)

Matthew 5:9 (NIV)

Matthew 6:3 (NKJV)

Ephesians 5:21 (NIV)

Recommended Reading

Philippians 4:6

Psalm 9 and Psalm 20

Recommended Reading

Philippians 4:6

Psalm 9 and Psalm 20